i KNOW MY BODY: BODY PARTS BABY BOOK

SPEEDY
PUBLISHING

Speedy Publishing LLC
40 E. Main St. #1156
Newark, DE 19711
www.speedypublishing.com

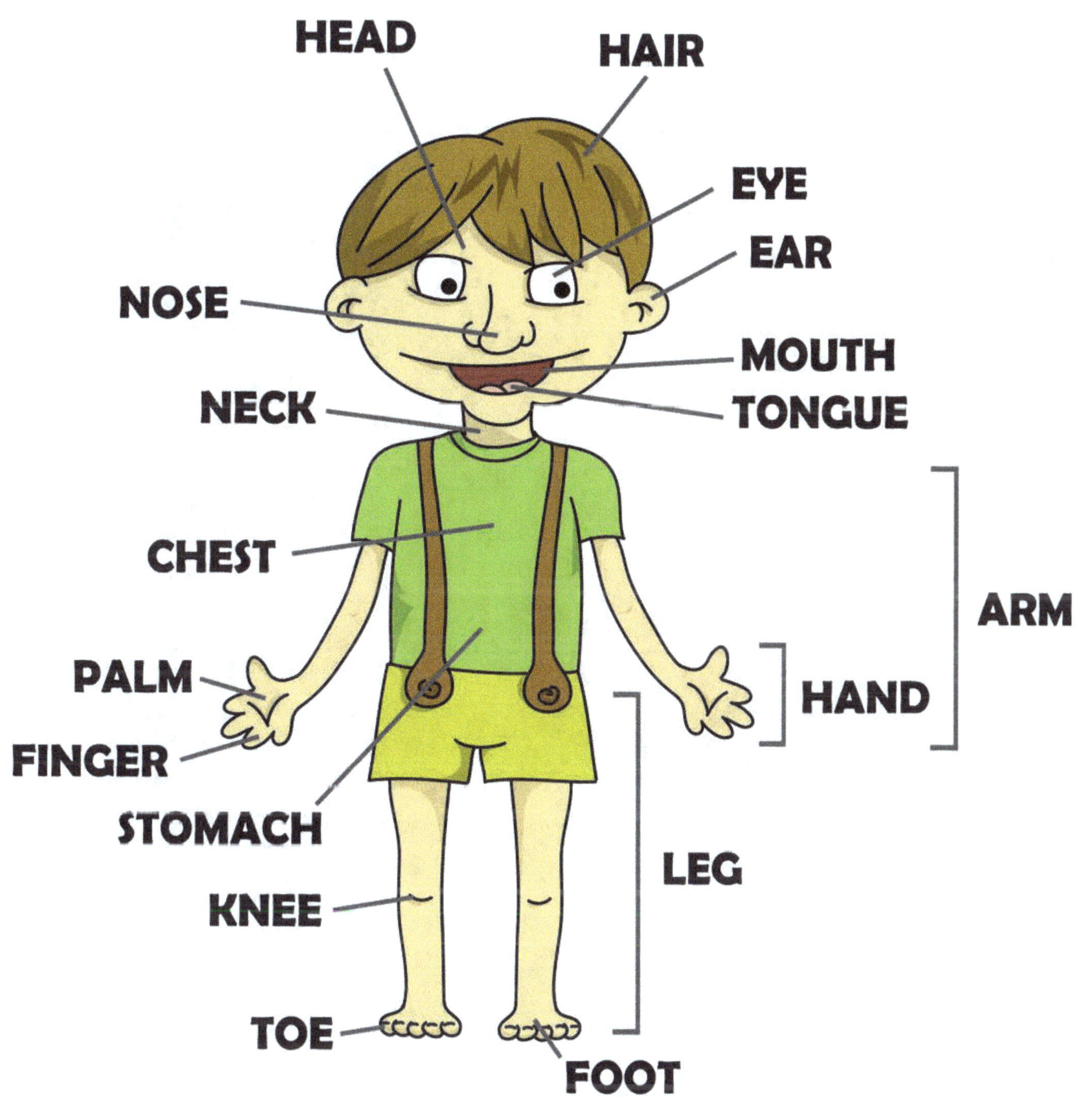

HEAD
HAIR
EYE
EAR
NOSE
MOUTH
TONGUE
NECK
CHEST
ARM
PALM
HAND
FINGER
STOMACH
LEG
KNEE
TOE
FOOT

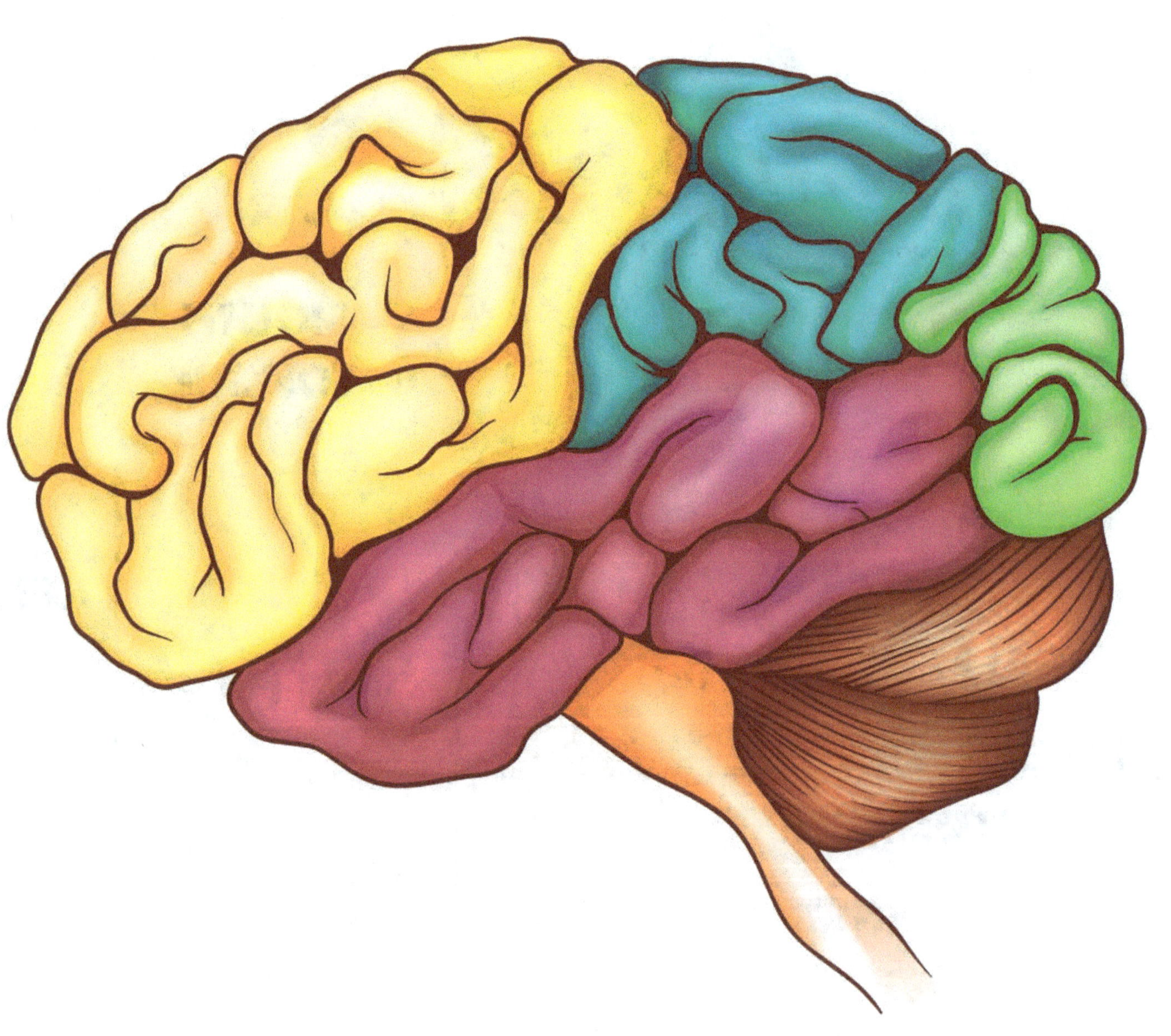

BRAIN

The average human brain is 3 lbs.

SKULL

The skull protects our internal organs
in our head specially the brain.

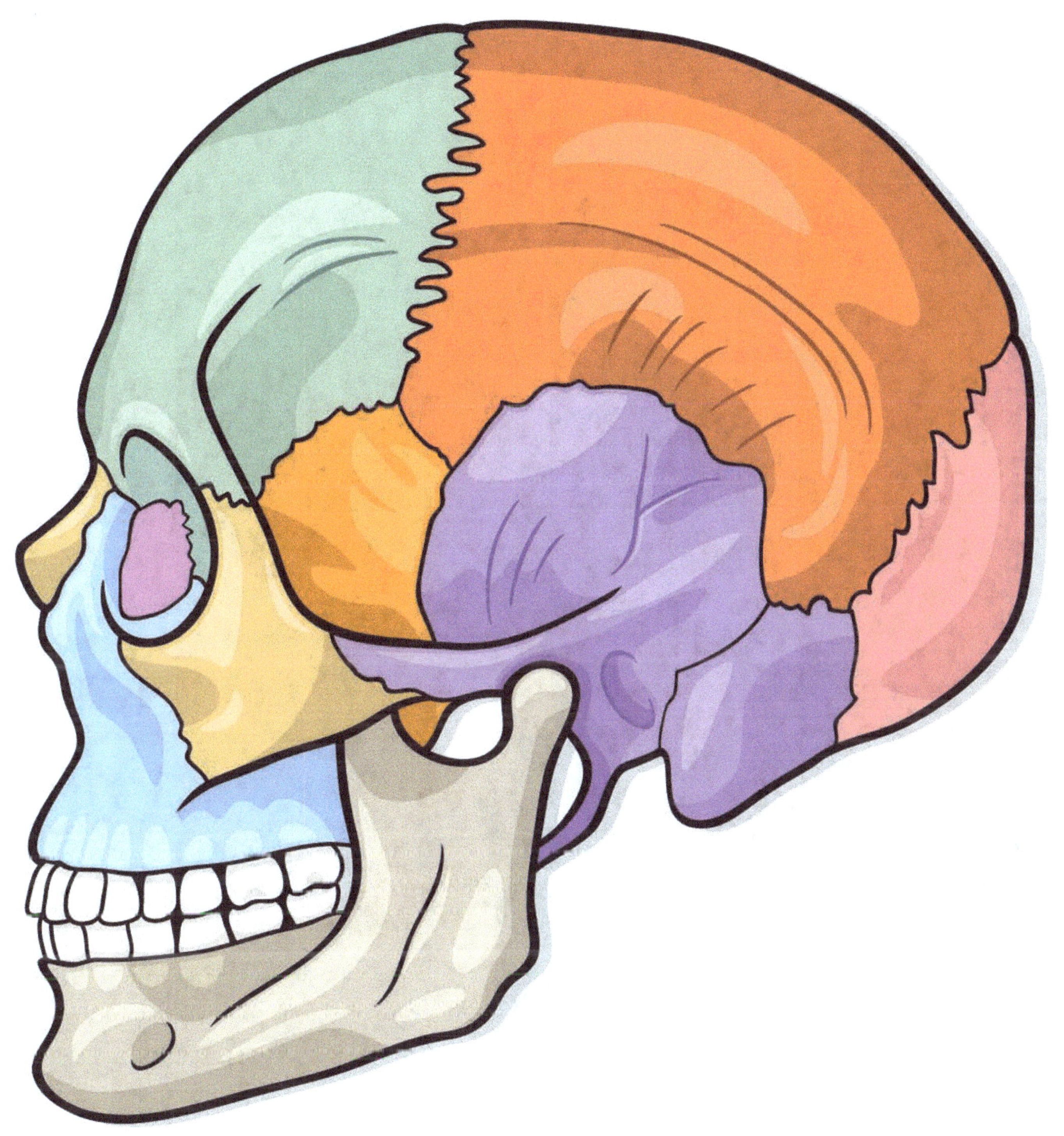

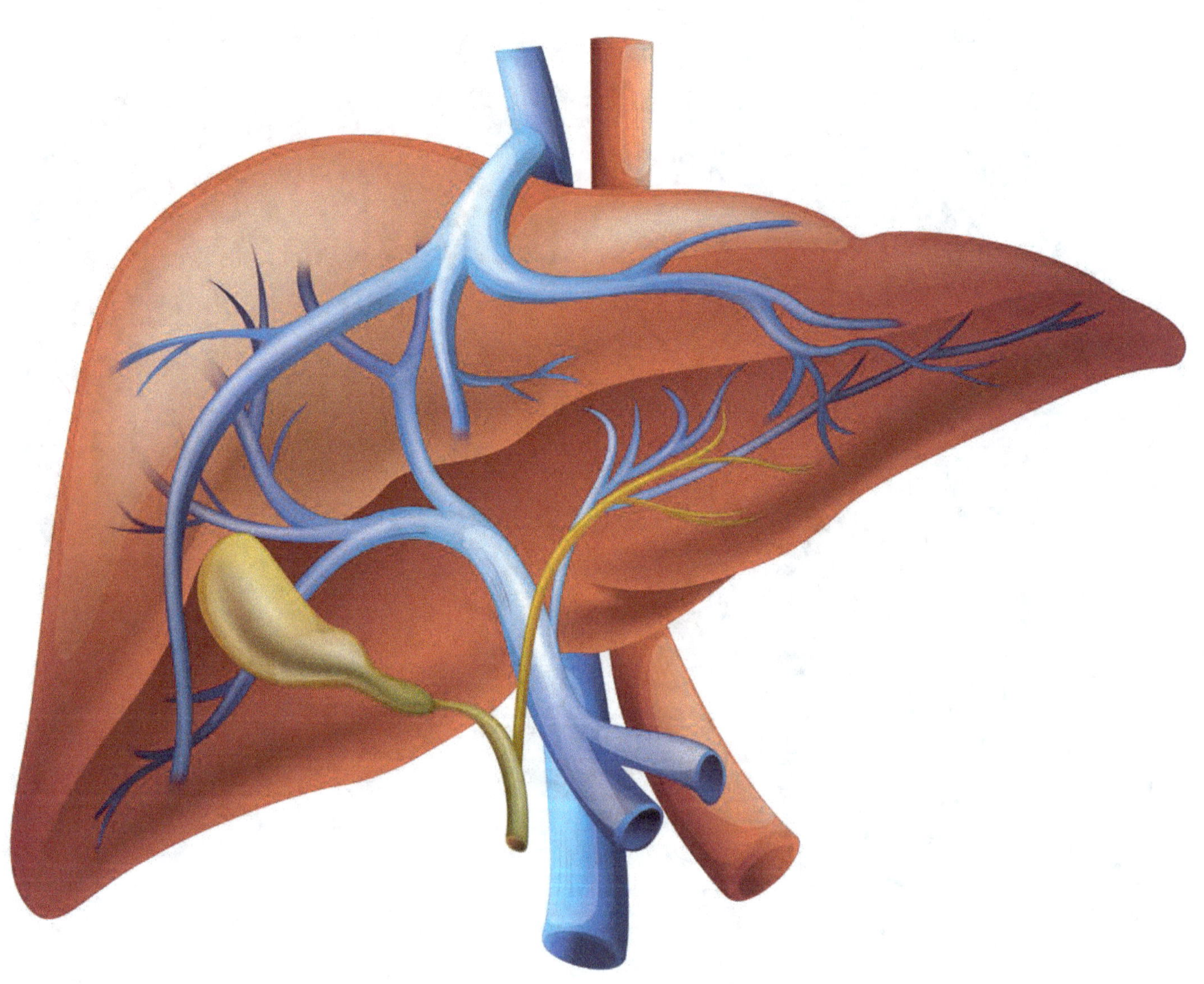

LIVER

The liver is the largest solid organ in our body. It's about 8 inches wide, 6.5 inches long and 4.5 inches thick and weighs approximately 3.5 pounds.

EYES

The human eye basically never changes size. However, when you're born, you can only see about 15 inches away.

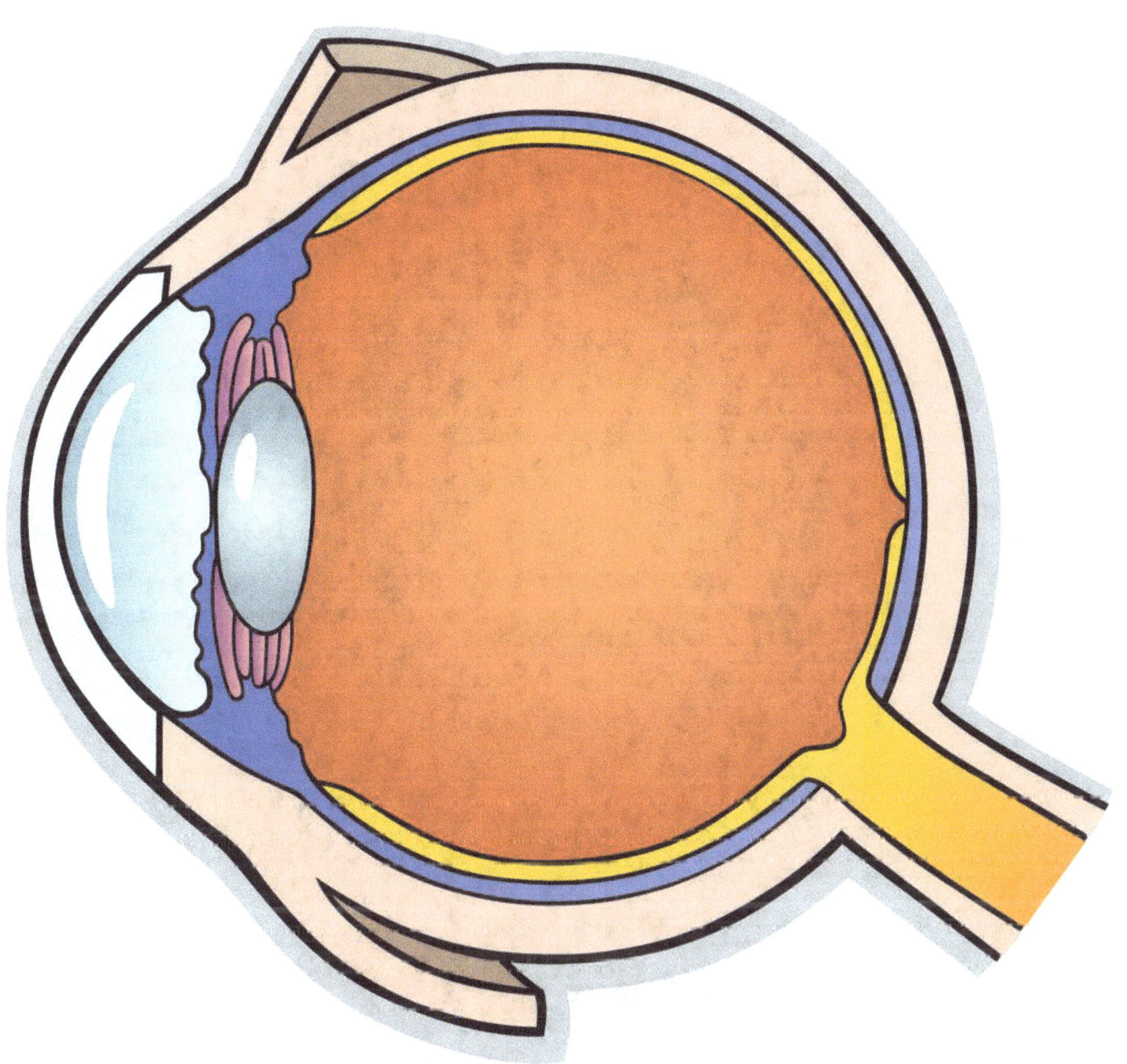

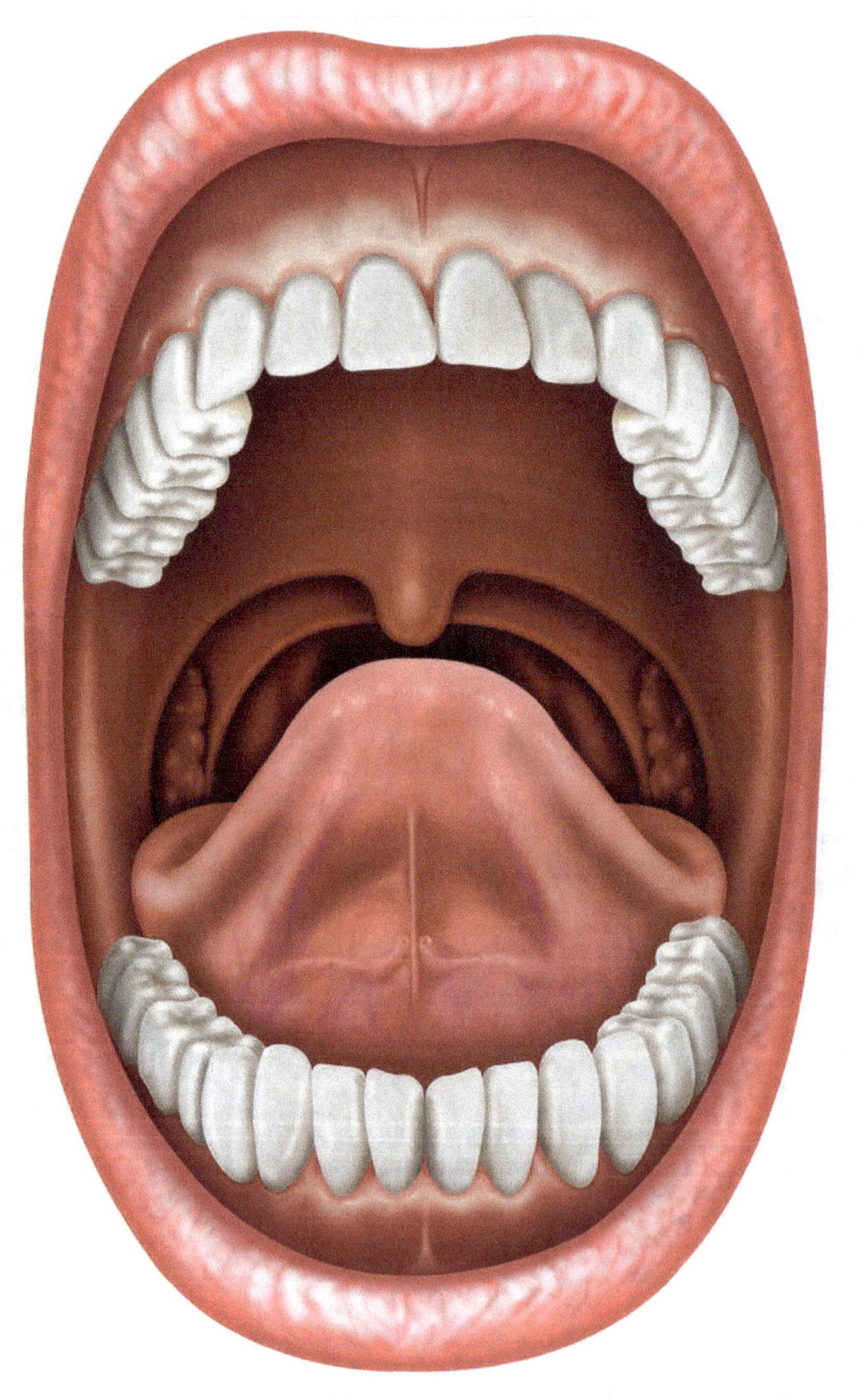

MOUTH

The mouth is the first portion of the alimentary canal that receives food and saliva.

TEETH

The first set (baby teeth) features 20 teeth.

The second set (adult teeth) features 32 teet.

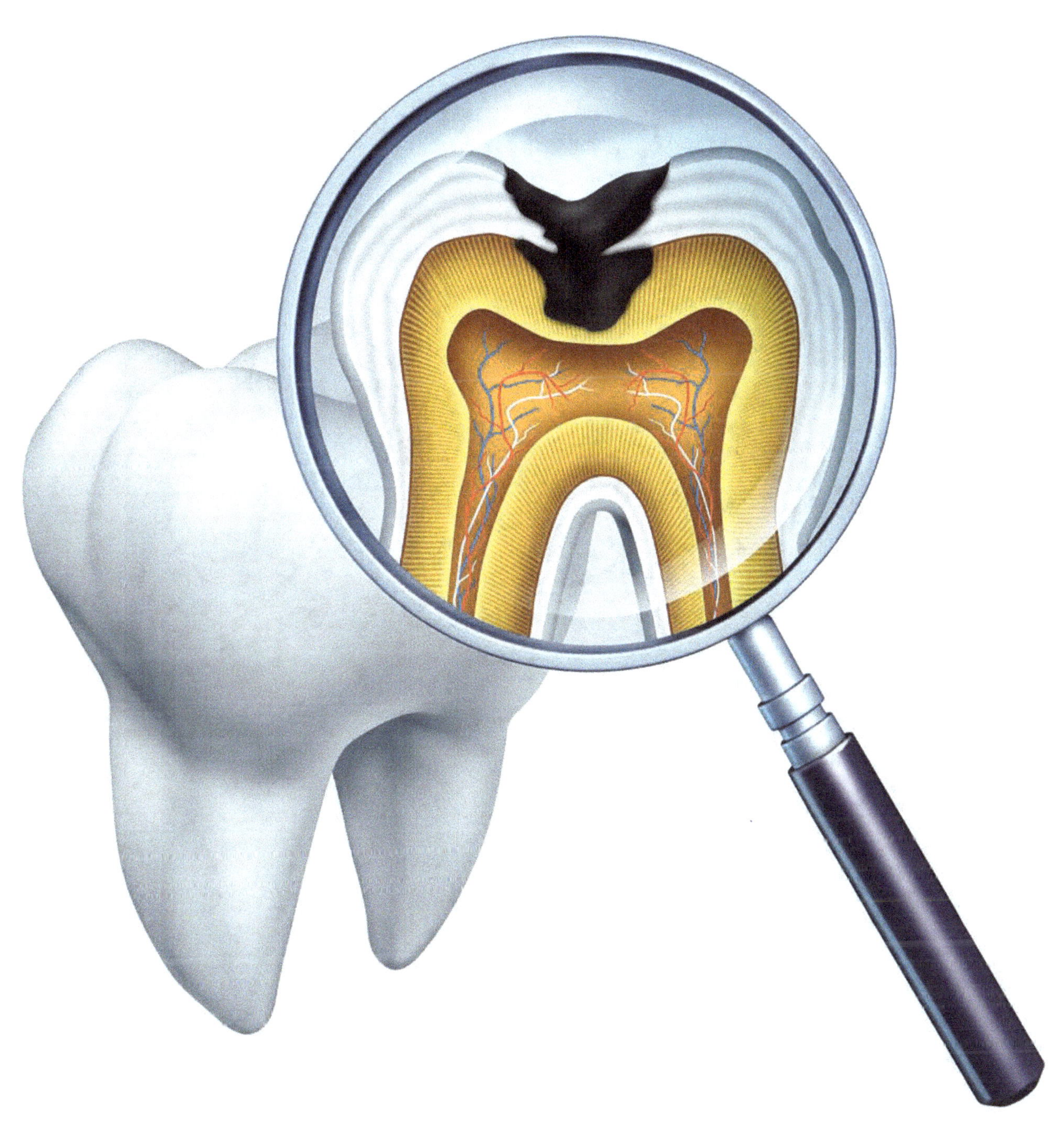

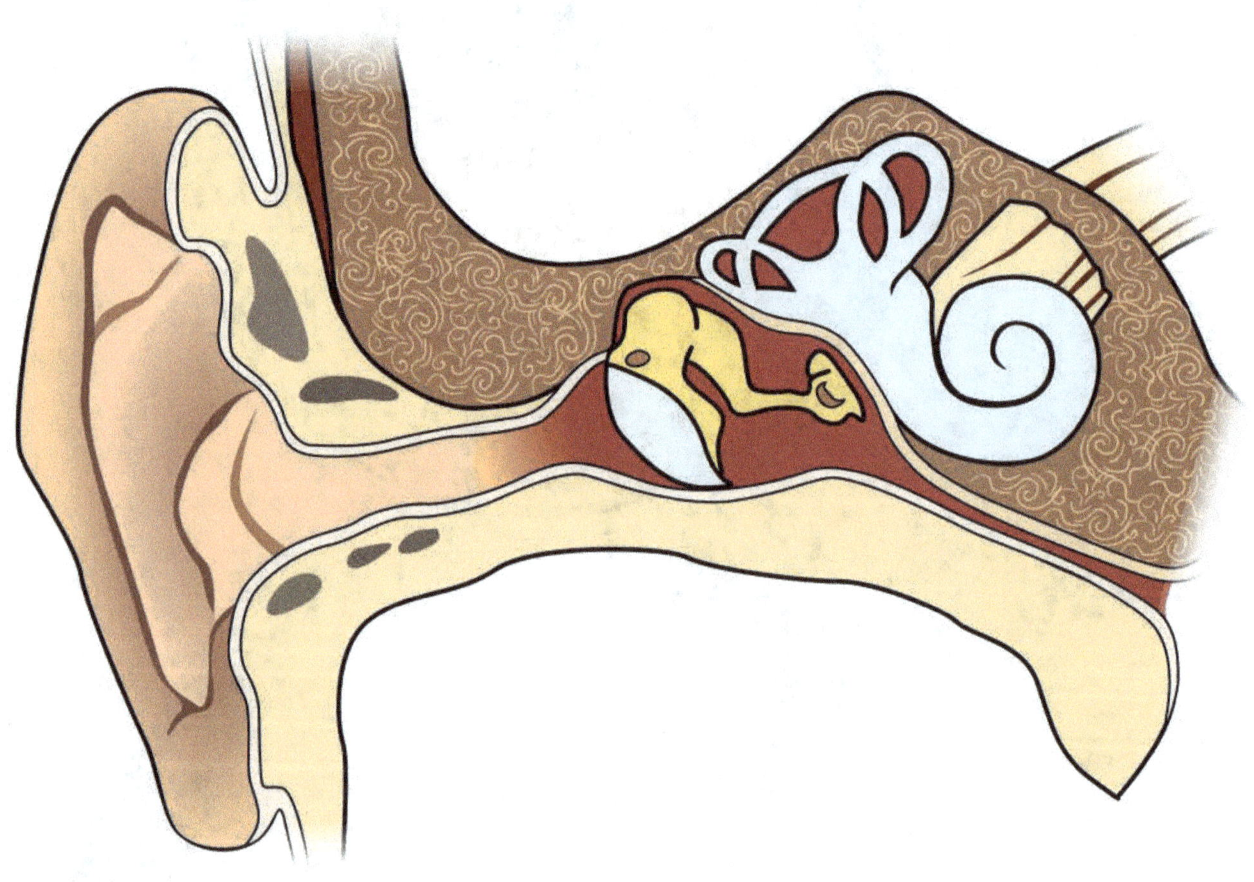

EAR

Ears convert sound waves into nerve impulses that are sent to the brain.

TONGUE

Almost half of the bacteria in your mouth live on your tongue.

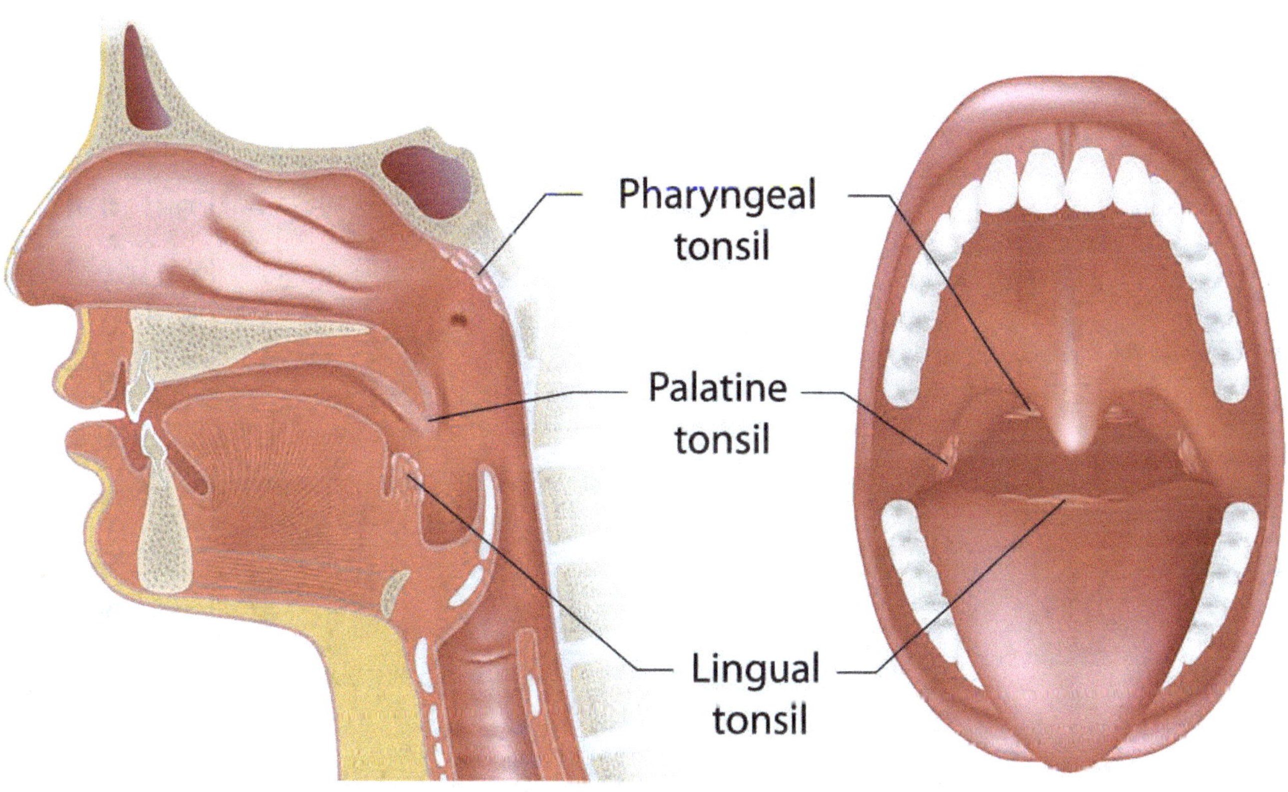

Pharyngeal tonsil
Palatine tonsil
Lingual tonsil

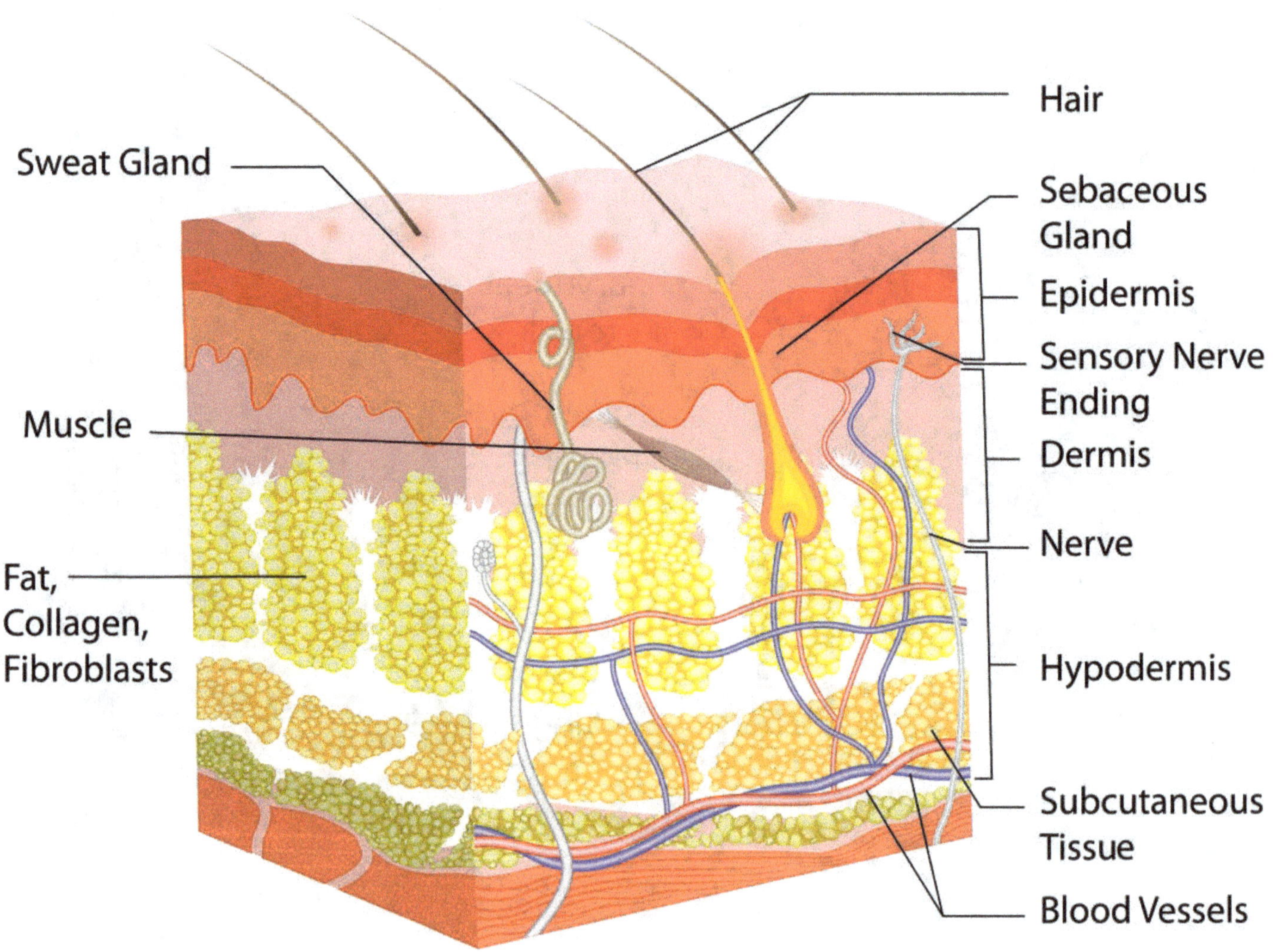

Hair
Sweat Gland
Sebaceous Gland
Epidermis
Sensory Nerve Ending
Muscle
Dermis
Fat, Collagen, Fibroblasts
Nerve
Hypodermis
Subcutaneous Tissue
Blood Vessels

SKiN

Skin is the body's largest organ.

STOMACH

People can survive without a stomach if it has to be removed due to some disease.

Esophagus
Lower Esophageal Sphincter
Cardia
Body of Stomach
Fundus
Muscularis
Longitudinal Layer
Circular Layer
Oblique Layer
Serosa
Pyloric Sphincter
Lesser Curvature
Mucosa
Duodenum
Duodenal Bulb
Greater Curvature
Pylorus
Gastric Rugae

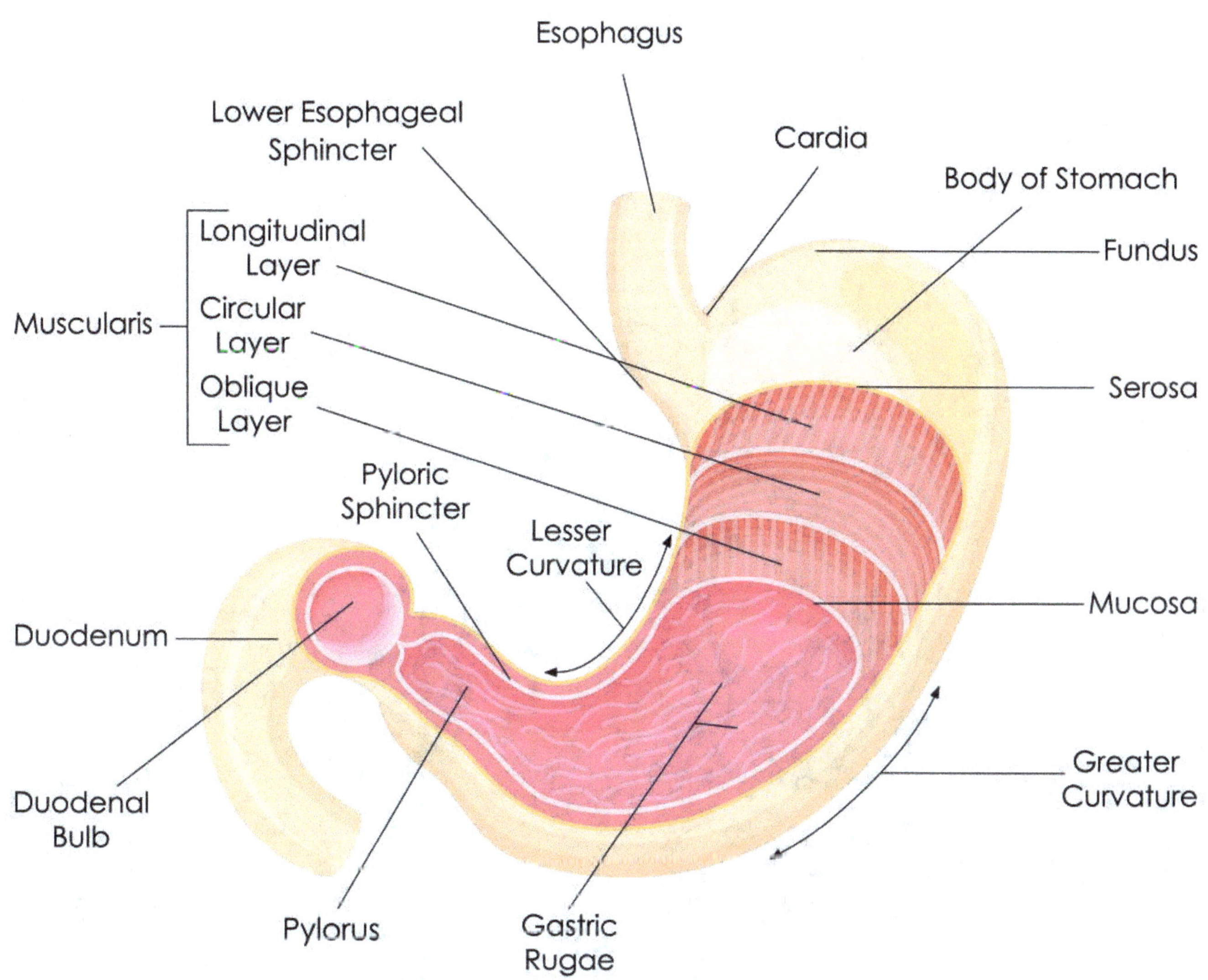

Stomach

FOOT

The 52 bones in your feet make up one quarter of all the bones in your body. When they are out of alignment, so is the rest of your body.

HEART

Your heart beats about 100,000 times in one day.

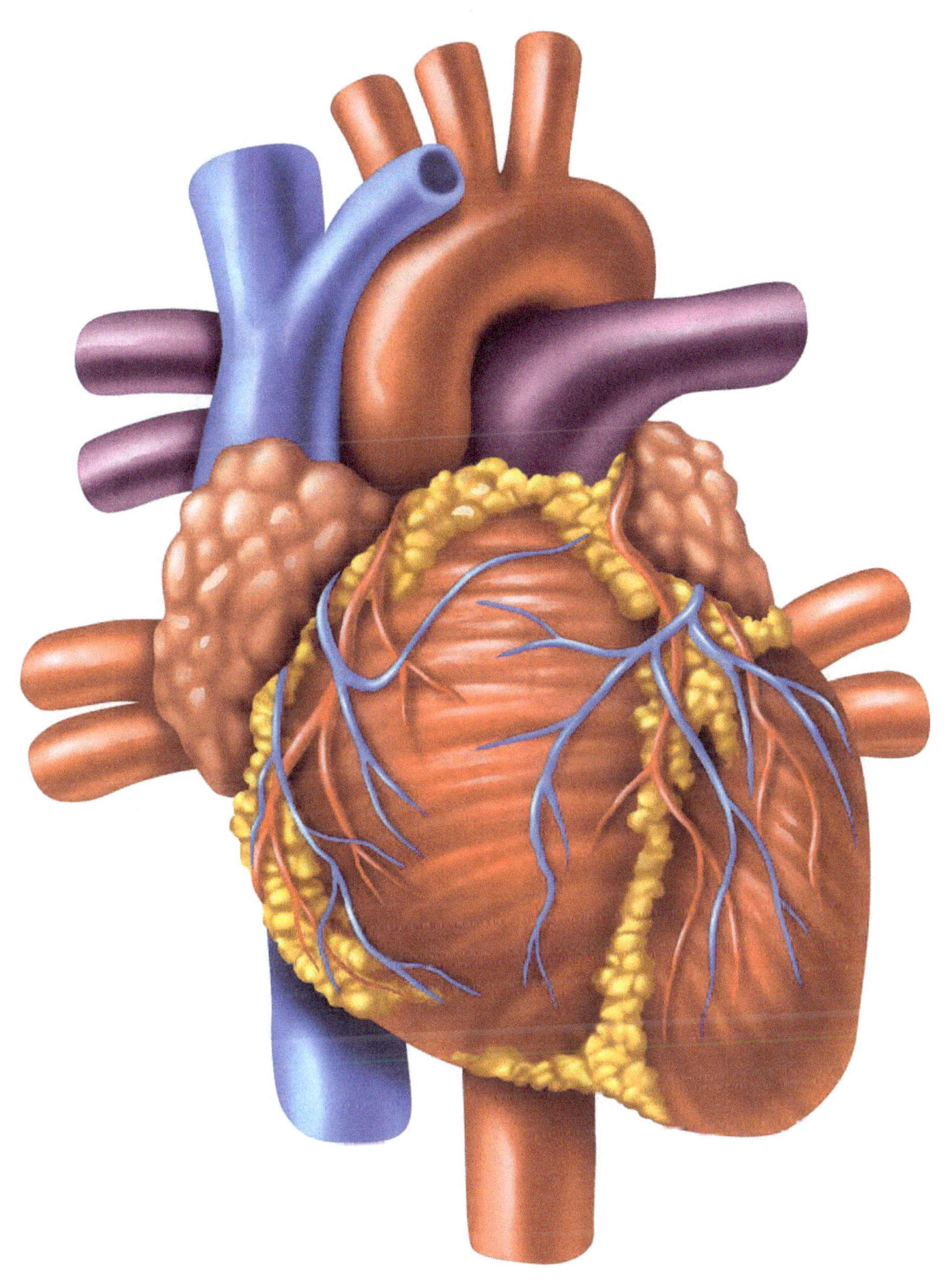

Human Respiratory System

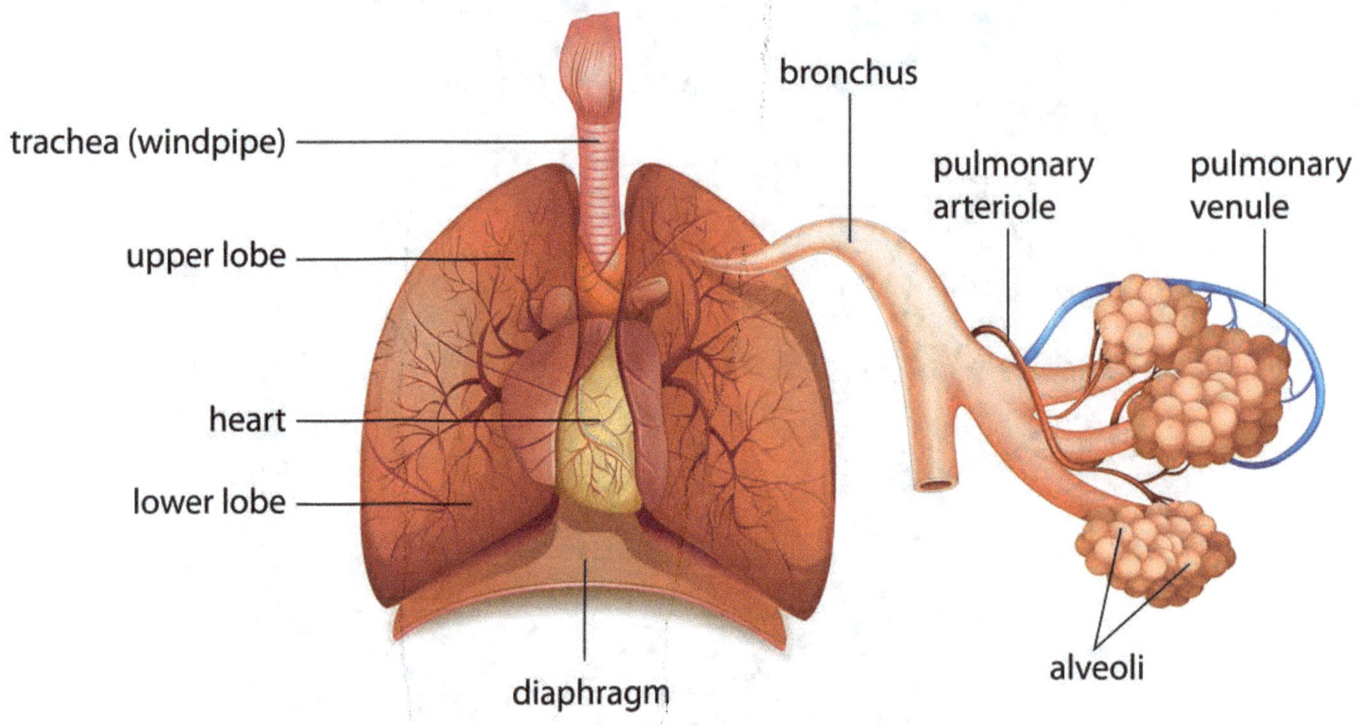

LUNGS

An average person breathes in around 11,000 litres of air every day.

KiDNEYS

The kidneys of a newborn baby are about 3X larger in proportion to body weight as in the adult.

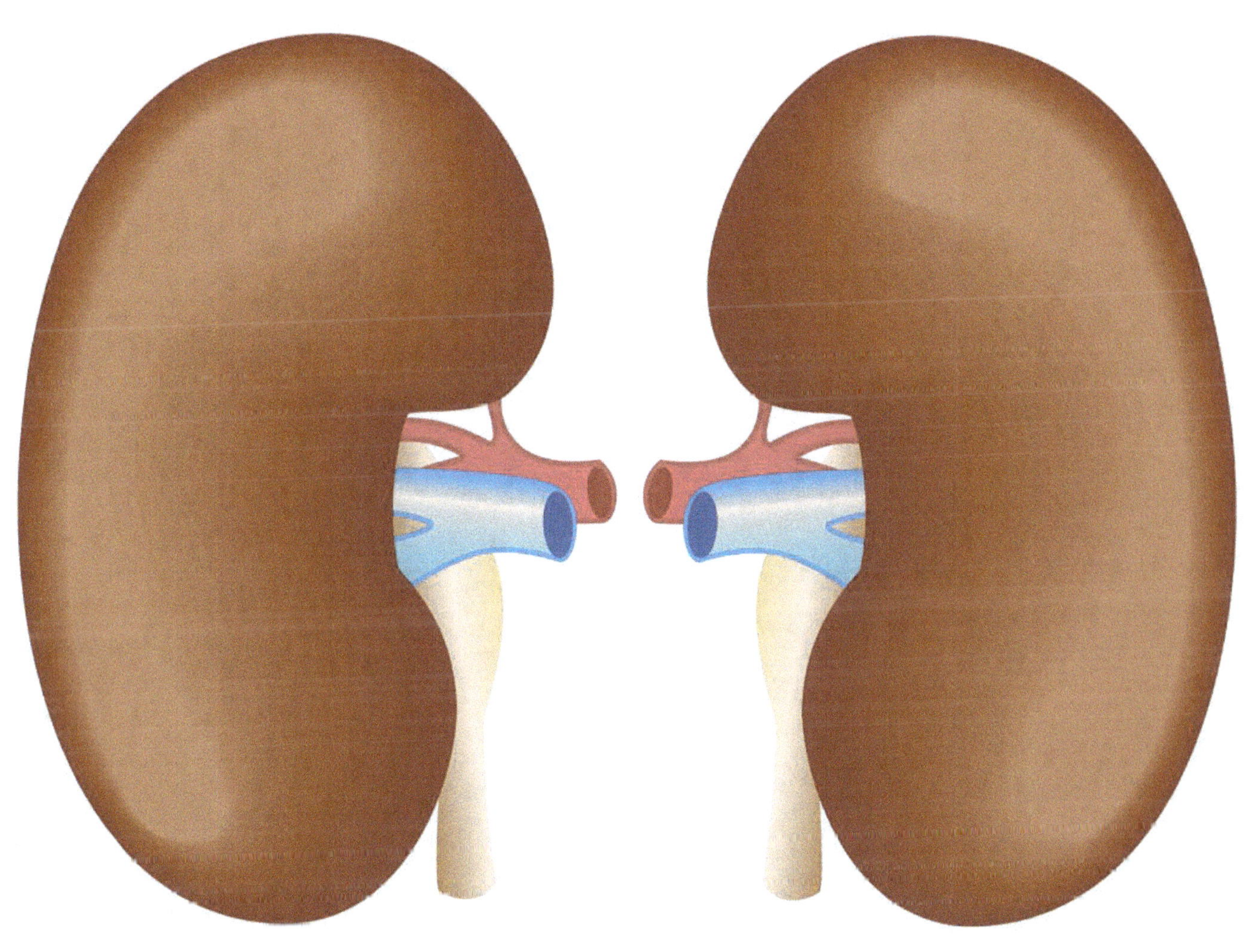